MOLLY PICON

A Gift of Laughter

Molly as Yonkele

MOLLY PICON

A Gift of Laughter

LILA PERL

Illustrated by Donna Ruff

THE JEWISH PUBLICATION SOCIETY

Philadelphia • New York 5750/1990

Library of Congress Cataloging-in-Publication Data

Perl, Lila.
  Molly Picon : a gift of laughter / Lila Perl : illustrated by Donna Ruff.
    p.   cm. — (The JPS young biography series)
  Summary: Follows the life and career of the Jewish entertainer
who performed in theater, movies, radio, and television for more
than eighty years.
  ISBN 0-8276-0336-3
  1. Picon, Molly—Juvenile literature.   2. Entertainers—United
States—Biography—Juvenile literature.   3. Jewish theater—History—
Juvenile literature.   4. Theater, Yiddish—History—Juvenile
literature. [1. Picon, Molly.   2. Entertainers.   3. Jews—
Biography.]   I. Ruff, Donna, ill.   II. Title.   III. Series.
PN2287.P53P47   1990
792'.028'092'B—dc20
[92]   *89-48421*
                                                          CIP
                                                          AC

Designed by Adrianne Onderdonk Dudden

10   9   8   7   6   5   4   3   2   1

CONTENTS

MOLLY
PICON

A Gift of Laughter

1

Baby Margaret

It's early evening in the bustling city of Philadelphia, way back in the year 1903. Through streets clogged with horse-drawn carts and carriages, one of the new electric trolley cars inches its way toward a street corner where a mother and a little girl stand waiting.

Most of the homeward-bound passengers sitting on the trolley's hard wooden benches have just finished a long day's work. They sit with nodding heads and glum, tired faces. But as the trolley clanks to a stop and the new passengers climb aboard, a few heads are raised.

Soon more and more of the passengers are looking up. Their eyes brighten. The tiny, elfin girl who has just entered the car with her mother has caught their interest. Who is this strange little creature? Why is she all dressed up in a ruffled costume and a small, pert hat? Where can she be going at this time of evening?

The little round-faced girl stares back at the other passengers through bold eyes, black as currants. For a while nobody says anything.

But finally a man leans forward on the moving trolley and speaks directly to the little girl. Maybe he's a bit more chatty than the others because he's recently had a whiskey or two at one of the city's corner saloons. In any case, he starts asking the questions that are on everybody's lips. . . .

Many, many times in her grown-up years, Molly Picon was to talk about how she made her acting debut on that Philadelphia trolley car at the age of five. When the friendly, slightly drunk passenger found out that Molly was on her way to the Bijou Theatre to try to win a five-dollar gold piece in a children's amateur-night contest, he urged her to give a dress-rehearsal performance right then and there on the trolley car.

Molly glanced at Mama Picon. Mama Picon glanced back with an expression that seemed to say, "Go ahead and show 'em, Molly."

Without a moment's hesitation, Molly launched into her act. It was a recitation and song, with lively gestures and dance steps, that ended with the lines:

"Baby dear, listen here,
I'm afraid to go home in the dark!"

The trolley-car audience exploded with applause, as Molly curtsied her finish. For a few magical moments, the weary passengers had forgotten their cares. Molly had

Five-year-old Molly on a Philadelphia trolley car

won their hearts and, as far as they were concerned, the amateur contest besides. The friendly passenger passed his hat around to take up a collection for the new little trouper.

Molly walked off the trolley car with one dollar and sixty cents, quite a lot of money in those days. And—as any of the people on the trolley might have predicted— she won the first prize of the five-dollar gold piece in the contest at the Bijou as well!

Later that evening, when Molly and her mother returned home and showed Molly's earnings to the rest of the family, Grandma had a suggestion. There might not always be an amateur contest around, with a five-dollar gold piece to win. But why not dress Molly up in her costume *every* evening and just have her ride around on the Philadelphia trolley cars?

Grandma was joking, of course. For even then it wasn't hard to guess that Molly was a natural-born entertainer with a real theater career ahead of her. From the time Molly was three or four, she'd been standing on her head, doing somersaults, reciting verses, and singing popular ditties. And the theater was already a second home to Molly because her mother worked as a seamstress, sewing costumes for the actresses who performed in Yiddish-language plays.

There were no baby-sitters during Molly's childhood, so Mama often had to take Molly and her younger sister, Helen, to the Yiddish theater with her. Rehearsals went on while Mama sewed, and Molly watched the actors from the wings or fell asleep on top of one of the wardrobe trunks.

Even the wandering life of an actor was already familiar to Molly by the time she was out of diapers. She'd been born in 1898—on June 1, according to Mama—in a walk-up building on Broome Street on New York City's Lower East Side. The building, with its small, cluttered apartments and its courtyard bathrooms shared by several families, was known as a tenement. It was typical of the dismal, congested quarters in which most poor Jewish families like the Picons—as well as other European immigrants—lived at that time.

Papa Picon, Molly's father, had come to America some years earlier from Poland and married Molly's mother. But Papa was the restless type. His regular job was as a shirtmaker in the small factories known as sweatshops, where people labored over their sewing machines for long hours each day. Often, though, Louis Picon tried other kinds of work, and sometimes he didn't work at all. His search for a life he would like took him and his family across the Hudson River to New Jersey and as far west as Chicago. By the time Molly was three, and the Picons were settled in Philadelphia, she had lived in a number of American cities.

Luckily for Molly, Philadelphia was a city with six or seven theaters. Many of them gave vaudeville shows, also advertised as "varieties." The varieties were a series of entertainments that really had nothing to do with each other. There might be an animal act, some skits or playlets, a comedian in baggy pants and a funny hat who told jokes, some song and dance numbers, an acrobat, and so on.

People flocked to the vaudeville theaters. Admission was fairly cheap and you could hiss the acts you didn't like and cheer the ones you did. Besides, where else could people go for entertainment in the early 1900s? Motion pictures were still in their infancy and television was undreamed of. The country's first movie theater had opened in Los Angeles as recently as 1902. And talking pictures—movies with sound—wouldn't be on the scene until 1927.

So vaudeville was in its heyday. And it was a perfect place for Molly to get her start. Some of the theaters were part of a chain. The same acts would be booked to travel around from theater to theater and city to city on what was known as a "vaudeville circuit." The local theater owners, though, were always trying to save money. So they would often hire "amateur acts" to perform, and pay them about fifty cents a night.

For Molly's act, she was billed as "Baby Margaret." This was the same stage name she had used when she'd won first prize in the competition at the Bijou.

In one "amateur" show after another, Molly sang, danced, and put her rubbery little body through the acrobatic tricks that came so easily to her. She soon became a special favorite with the vaudeville audiences. Probably many wondered if she was a forty-year-old midget or a real live six-year-old. But they adored her either way. The energy and love of entertaining that radiated from her made people feel good.

Along about this time, Molly also began appearing with the Yiddish-language company at the theater where her mother was the wardrobe mistress. The Jewish plays were often tearful family stories in which there were lots of poor orphans. Molly and her sister Helen easily slipped into these children's parts. The "acting" was mostly babyish weeping and wailing.

But soon Molly was given real acting parts. She and little Helen appeared in a Yiddish version of the famous American anti-slavery story *Uncle Tom's Cabin*. Helen played Little Eva, the rich planter's daughter. And Molly sang, jigged, and spoke an imperfect Yiddish in the role of the mischievous black child, Topsy.

Molly had by now entered grade school and one of the big problems for seven-year-old Molly was getting up in time for class in the morning. Some of the performances Molly acted in didn't end until after midnight. She couldn't fit in a nap after school either. She usually had to go directly to the theater to rehearse, then home to dinner, and then back to the theater to get into her makeup and costume.

Nobody thought of hiring a special tutor for Molly instead of sending her to school. The family couldn't have afforded the expense. In fact, the money that Molly earned was needed to help out at home.

Papa wasn't around much of the time. And even when he was, he would often be busy teaching himself Greek or reading great Russian writers like Tolstoy and Dostoyevsky. Sadly, Papa didn't take much interest in Molly's blossoming stage career. It was Mama whose warm, generous spirit stood behind Molly and cheered her on.

By the time Molly was nine or ten, a new kind of entertainment that combined movies *and* vaudeville had become popular. Theaters called "nickelodeons" showed a short, jumpy, black-and-white motion film and a live stage act for which they charged a nickel. The films were "silents," of course. The words the actors spoke were written on the screen. And the action was accom-

Performing the kazatsky *at age ten*

panied by piano music played live in the theater, along-
side the movie screen.

Molly's "Baby Margaret" act was just right for the
nickelodeon audiences, in which there were lots of children. She sang "I'm Afraid to Go Home in the
Dark," recited a poem about a Dutch boy who had a
twin brother and didn't know which one of the twins he
was, and performed a lively Russian dance called a *kazatsky.* Only a little acrobat like Molly could have managed to keep her balance as she hopped about the stage
in a squatting position, rapidly tossing one leg and then
the other out in front of her.

Little was the right word for Molly. At school, her gymnasium teacher would call out the heights of her classmates as she measured them. At the age of twelve, most of the girls were around five feet tall. But Molly was only a little over four feet. She entered her teens, but still she didn't sprout. Even as a grown-up, Molly never reached five feet. Throughout her adult career, the petite actress measured four feet, eleven inches and weighed about one hundred pounds.

But Molly's small stature was part of what made her the lively sprite that audiences loved. The real problem, as Molly entered high school, was how to balance the demands of a stage life and an education. There didn't seem to be enough hours in the day to both perform and study. And then there was the constant need for money. Few poor immigrant families could support a child through high school in those days. And Molly's family was no exception. Many youngsters worked at full-time jobs by the time they were fourteen, or even younger.

Molly tried her best anyway. But the long trip to high school each day combined with her vaudeville bookings in Philadelphia—and sometimes in cities as far away as Baltimore and Washington—soon began to take their toll. How could she manage it all and keep on helping Mama out with her earnings?

By her second year in high school, Molly had come to a painful decision. In order to devote herself to trying to make a real success on the stage, she would have to say good-bye to formal learning. Mama supported Molly's decision. She agreed that perhaps Molly would even be lucky enough to get on one of the big vaudeville circuits and travel all over the country at a regular weekly salary.

In 1915, two years short of graduation and well aware of the bumpy road that lay ahead, Molly left William Penn High School in Philadelphia. She was sixteen. It was time to throw herself wholeheartedly into the work she loved best in all the world.

2

A Jewish Peter Pan

Had Molly made a terrible mistake in leaving high school? The first couple of years were difficult. Molly appeared in plays and in variety shows in and around Philadelphia. But she still wasn't making a lot more money than when she was nine and doing her successful "Baby Margaret" act in the nickelodeons.

Papa was less and less on the scene. And Mama, who was still working long hours at sewing costumes, needed help meeting the installments due on the furniture and paying the rent on the little house in Philadelphia. Molly *had* to do something to boost her income.

One day in 1917, she bravely walked into the office of one of the hard-boiled agents who put together touring acts for the vaudeville circuits. World War I had broken out

13

in Europe in 1914, and now in April of 1917 the United States had joined England, France, and the other Allied nations in their fight against Germany and Austria-Hungary. A new and very popular song of the day was "There's a Long, Long Trail A-Winding into the Land of My Dreams." It was a touching and beautiful melody with words that told of a soldier's yearning to return to his loved one and to a world at peace.

Molly had only to sing a little bit of the song and to show off some of her other talents such as playing the ukulele and tumbling like a circus clown. In a few days' time, she had the "big break" she'd been hoping for. She was booked to travel around the country on one of the major vaudeville circuits.

The act that Molly was to be part of was called "The Four Seasons." Each of the young women in the act represented a different season of the year. Molly, the smallest of the group, was Winter because she was able to do a Russian dance, the *kazatsky*, that she had performed in her childhood nickelodeon days.

This was Molly's first time "on the road," away from Mama for months and months at a time, traveling as far west as San Francisco. "Nice girls" didn't go around without a chaperone in those days. But the theater was a world that made its own demands—and besides, Mama Picon had faith in Molly. She knew that Molly would behave properly, and she did.

Molly learned a lot on her first tour and became toughened to the life of a traveling actor. "The Four Seasons" journeyed from place to place by train and usually stayed at grimy small hotels or in boardinghouses near the railroad station or the local theater. To keep expenses down, the three younger members of the group shared a room that was always cluttered with their costumes, makeup, and stage props. But all four looked out for one another, and the others kept an eye on the less-experienced Molly.

Members of some of the other traveling acts on the same circuit also became Molly's friends and teachers. There was an acrobatic troupe, a trained-seal act, a magic act, and several others typical of vaudeville entertainment of the time. Molly was earning enough money to send about half her salary—fifteen or twenty dollars—home to Mama each week.

But, like all good things, Molly's wartime touring career was to run into a snag. She had been on the road about six months when the great influenza epidemic of 1918 broke out and soon ran rampant all across the country. The killer flu had first struck in war-torn Europe and quickly traveled to America. In all, some twenty million people were to die of the disease.

Those who had not so far been felled by the flu were warned to avoid public gathering places. One by one, the cities into which "The Four Seasons" and the other acts were booked were closing their schools, stores, and theaters. Molly's money began to dwindle, as the group traveled from town to town unable to give performances.

The early winter of 1918 found Molly and her act stranded in the city of Boston. There, too, the theaters had been shut down—all, that is, but one. It had an impressive name: the Grand Opera House. At one time, famous American actors like the Barrymores had played there. But now the neighborhood around the theater had become run-down and ugly. A noisy elevated train regularly clattered back and forth overhead, and the theater was used mainly for wrestling matches and for weekend performances of Yiddish plays.

As soon as Molly heard about the Yiddish plays, she set out for the not-so-grand Grand Opera House. She was the only Jew in "The Four Seasons" act. Maybe she would find a Yiddish actor from Philadelphia who knew her or Mama and who would lend her the money to get home. For by now Molly was really broke.

Years later, Molly said that the only reason the poor old Grand Opera House hadn't been closed down was that it was so unimportant the Boston health authorities didn't even know it was there. She also had to admit that the flu epidemic of 1918, terrible though it was for so many, had brought her luck.

The manager of the Yiddish theater company turned out to be a young Polish Jew named Jacob Kalich. He had immigrated to America just four years earlier and still spoke a heavily accented English. But Molly's hunch was right. He *had* caught one of her performances in Philadelphia and remembered her lively talent. Instead of giving Molly the money to return home, he offered her a job with his Yiddish theater company. He needed a soubrette—a vivacious young singer, dancer, and comedienne—who could perform in Yiddish, because the company's regular soubrette was down with the flu.

Molly didn't have to think twice. She accepted. Kalich advanced her some money to pay for her boardinghouse lodgings in Boston, and Molly tearfully parted company with the other three members of "The Four Seasons." They were happy for Molly because a job was a job. But they were also probably baffled about her up-

Molly sharpening her acrobatic skills on the vaudeville circuit

coming role on the Yiddish stage. Even Molly wasn't quite sure of what was expected of her. In the past she *had* performed in Yiddish plays. But her recent experience had been in American vaudeville. She didn't think of herself as a Yiddish actress. Jacob Kalich, she would learn, was to change all that.

The manager of Molly's new theater company had been born in 1891 into a religious family. His father, grandfather, and great-grandfather had been rabbis, and young Jacob, too, was studying for the rabbinate. But at the age of fifteen something happened that changed his life.

A troupe of traveling Yiddish actors came through Jacob's home town of Rymanov, in Poland. He became friendly with them and, when they asked to borrow his long, black, rabbinical student's coat for use as a stage costume, he agreed. Somehow, when the actors moved on to the next town they took along not only Jacob's coat, but Jacob as well.

Just as Molly had made the decision to leave school for the stage, so Jacob gave up his religious studies for the life of an actor, writer, director, and theater manager. After touring Europe in Yiddish plays, appearing in cities from the Romanian capital of Bucharest to Paris and London, Jacob had made his way to America.

As Molly began working with the new company, she met her fellow actors. Among them was the young Paul Muni who was to become famous on Broadway and in Hollywood. Another member of the troupe was Menashe Skulnick who was to act in both Yiddish and American theater, usually portraying a meek, blundering comedy character.

Molly was rushed into the substitute role of the soubrette practically overnight. Could she learn her lines fast enough? Would the audience compare her unfavorably with the actress she was replacing? How would her vaudeville songs, stories, and jokes come across in Yiddish translation?

Molly needn't have worried. The moment she stepped out on the stage her magic went to work. She had only to be herself—the Molly who loved to make people laugh—to capture hearts across the footlights. She was a hit, and the entire company celebrated with her at an opening-night party.

Jacob Kalich knew he had a star and he began to write new roles for Molly. But what kinds of parts could a tiny, almost tomboyish actress play? As theater critics would soon describe her, Molly was a "Peter Pan" type. She could easily have portrayed the boy in the very popular English play of that name who refused to grow up and whose life was a succession of youthful pranks and adventures.

The popular Yiddish-theater actresses of the day were almost the exact opposite of Molly. Most of them had imposing figures and fleshy bodies. They played serious, dramatic roles as long-suffering or self-sacrificing heroines. These were the women whose names were up in lights on New York City's Second Avenue, the famous Yiddish theater district to which Jewish audiences thronged for entertainment.

Jacob realized that slim, dark-haired, impish Molly couldn't compete in the emotional, chest-heaving parts that the "great ladies" performed. So his inventive mind went to work writing new plays for Molly to appear in.

*Molly and Yonkel announce their engagement
to an audience of well-wishers.*

One of them, *Yonkele*, was to be among her most famous roles. Twenty-year-old Molly played a thirteen-year-old yeshiva boy, a Jewish religious-school student, who wants to grow up fast and solve all the world's problems. Molly's *Yonkele* costume was a peaked black cap, a white shirt and stockings, a black tie, black pumps, and a long black coat. Paul Muni, who was only a couple of years older than Molly, played her grouchy old father.

Yonkele earned Molly the nickname of the "Jewish Peter Pan." Had any Yiddish actress ever played a teenage boy before, or done it so convincingly? As Molly clowned and danced her way through Jacob Kalich's other new productions for her, she realized how well he understood how to use her abilities. She also became aware that their working relationship was developing into something more personal—a romantic one.

Their backgrounds, however, were quite different. Jacob was still very European in his outlook. He spoke several languages, including an excellent Yiddish. But his English was poor. Molly, in fact, had first thought of him as a "greenhorn" and secretly criticized his clothes and his accent. For Molly thought of herself as a "born American."

But now, as the two spent more time together, she began to respond to his charm, warmth, and intelligence, and to admire his serious but smiling good looks. Soon he was no longer "Mr. Kalich" or even "Jacob" to Molly. He was the more familiar "Yonkel"— his first name in Yiddish. Before long, Molly accepted his proposal of marriage.

Molly and Yonkel actually celebrated their engagement on the stage of Boston's Grand Opera House, after one of the regular performances. The audience paid a slightly higher ticket price to witness the special event and to shout "Mazel tov!" meaning "Good luck!" Mama Picon, who had traveled up from Philadelphia some time earlier, was present at the festivities, too.

By now World War I had ended with the signing of an armistice on November 11, 1918, and the flu epidemic was beginning to die down. It seemed a good time to look to the future. So on June 29, 1919, Molly and Yonkel were married in the back room of the little grocery store in Philadelphia that Yonkel had bought for Mama Picon.

The wedding was small and modest, but Yonkel made no secret of the big plans he had for Molly. He had made up his mind that he was going to find a way to make his "Jewish Peter Pan" a famous performer on New York's busy, glittering Second Avenue.

3

The Sweetheart of Second Avenue

Second Avenue! It was the "Broadway" that Yiddish actors everywhere dreamed of conquering in the early 1900s. What made it so popular was the huge Jewish immigrant population that had been flocking to America since the 1880s. The newcomers had been fleeing Russia and other parts of Eastern Europe to escape poverty, lack of opportunity, military service, and the dreaded massacres of Jews that were known as pogroms.

New York City was the main port of entry to the "golden land," where Jews hoped to find a better life. Many settled on Manhattan's Lower East Side. They lived in the dark, overcrowded tenements and worked at whatever jobs they could find—in the needle trades, as cigarette- and cigar-makers, as street peddlers of all sorts.

Their earnings were small. But Second Avenue and other Lower Manhattan streets offered theaters, music halls, and cafés where people could meet and relax. Even if it meant going without one of the necessities, the immigrants felt it was worth saving up for a theater ticket to hear the music and the language they loved, to lose themselves in a drama or laugh at a comedy. Above all, the audiences were entranced with the popular actors of the Second Avenue theater. They followed their heroes in their starring roles and took a keen interest in their private lives as well.

Would Molly ever make it to the Second Avenue stage? Back in Boston after their marriage, she and Yonkel continued giving performances at the Grand Opera House and on local tours to other parts of New England. Even when Molly became pregnant, she went on playing her bouncy, frisky roles, doing somersaults until she was in her seventh month of pregnancy. Only then did Molly leave the stage to wait for the birth of her child. She hoped, too, that soon afterward the long-awaited invitation to appear on Second Avenue would be offered her.

But Molly and Yonkel were to be disappointed in both of their expectations. The more tragic blow was the loss of their child, a little girl who was born dead after a difficult home delivery. It was the year 1920, and hospital births were not as common as they would later become. Even sadder, Molly soon learned that she would never be able to have children.

If the Second Avenue theater owners had begun to clamor for Molly at this point, it would have helped to lift her crushed spirits. But Yonkel still had been unable to get her a booking. So, to take Molly as far away as possible from her troubles and at the same time further her career, Yonkel came up with a wonderful idea. He would take Molly to Europe and make a star of her there.

Almost all of the actors, writers, and directors of the Second Avenue theater had gotten their start in Europe. There were famous troupes in Lithuania, Poland, and Romania that toured the continent playing to Jewish audiences. Yonkel himself had many contacts abroad from his own touring years. Once European theater-goers got a taste of Molly, Yonkel figured, they would write to their relatives in America. And their praises would create a growing appetite for the sparkling, petite entertainer, back home in the very city of her birth.

Yonkel's plan to revive Molly's spirits had an almost immediate effect. The excitement of a sea voyage followed by an engagement to play *Yonkele* at the Yiddish theater in Paris was just the tonic she needed. Soon Molly and Yonkel were on their way to Poland where again she opened in *Yonkele*. Molly also acted in other comedies that Yonkel had written, often playing a ragamuffin or a little scamp, doing her funny songs and showing off her dancing and acrobatic talents.

In Poland, Molly and Yonkel visited with Yonkel's mother, to whom he had been writing and sending money since he had left home at fifteen. Meeting Yonkel's mother and witnessing the reunion between mother and son deeply touched Molly. Sadly, Yonkel's father, the rabbi, had died by this time. Molly and Yonkel then traveled on to Austria, Czechoslovakia, and Romania. One of the goals of the trip had been for Molly to improve her Yiddish, which she did with Yonkel as her teacher.

In most of the European cities where Molly performed, she was a new kind of actress with new material. Audiences were used to more serious plays. But they soon began to accept the light roles that Molly did so well. She could also play comedy with a slightly sad twist, as in *Mamele*, or "Little Mother." *Mamele* was the story of a young girl whose mother dies, leaving her to look after her older sisters and brothers. Although still a child herself, she keeps house for her "children," worries about them, comforts them, and gives them advice. Molly was endearing in this role and her audiences adored her.

More than two years went by, with Molly becoming better known and loved everywhere in Europe. At last it was time to return to America. Was Second Avenue ready for Molly? Molly had worked hard and her expectations were high.

Back in New York, the theater managers that Yonkel talked to were at first hesitant. Did people *really* know who Molly Picon was? Would they buy tickets? Grudgingly, one of them finally agreed to put Molly on for a weekend of playing *Yonkele*. The theater posters announcing the performances went up. The box office put the tickets on sale. Molly and the cast went into rehearsals. It was now or never.

Molly's weekend on Second Avenue was to stretch into a lengthy career. Just as Yonkel had predicted, word of mouth from Europe created an immediate audience for Molly. Long before the first performance, lines began forming to buy tickets. People's relatives had written them from cities as far away as Paris and even Warsaw not to miss Molly when she came to New York.

Crowds line up for tickets to see Molly perform Yonkele.

The theater management had no choice but to keep her on for an extended engagement.

In the months and years that followed, Molly appeared in plays with titles like *Tzipke, Shmendrik, Gypsy Girl, Little Devil, Raizele,* and, of course, *Mamele,* which had so charmed audiences abroad. To keep people coming back for repeat performances, Molly always worked something new into a role. She would do a sequence of tap dancing or toe dancing, add cartwheels and splits, perform a trapeze or tightrope act, enter on a horse, do a fearless high-dive into a tank! She would play the ocarina, the concertina, the xylophone, the violin, or one of the other eight instruments that were among her skills. She kept her audiences goggle-eyed. They never knew what was coming next. Molly had truly earned the name by which everyone now knew her. She was the "Sweetheart of Second Avenue."

Molly was already familiar with the frankness and openness of the Yiddish-theater audiences of America. On Second Avenue they seemed even more lively. From the start, the Yiddish theater had attracted working men and women, old grandmothers in head shawls, mothers with babies in their arms. People brought along homemade snacks in brown paper bags to eat during the performance, or bought soda water, candy, or fruit from shouting vendors at the intermission. They sometimes chatted or made comments while the curtain was up. And between the acts they mingled freely and exchanged the latest news and gossip, almost like people at a family reunion. Most of all, they let the actors know how they felt with loud applause, cheers, and whistles—and sometimes with hisses and boos.

By 1923, when Molly made her Second Avenue debut, immigration to the United States had begun to drop off because of recent government restrictions. But the Jewish audiences were still avid for Yiddish theater. Some had by now moved away from Lower Manhattan to newer and better neighborhoods in the Bronx or Brooklyn, or across the river to New Jersey. Theaters sprang up in the new Jewish communities, and the "Sweetheart of Second Avenue" made the rounds appearing in them.

Back home on Second Avenue, business continued to thrive, largely because of theater parties. Audiences were growing a little more prosperous and would purchase tickets that had been bought up in large blocks by charitable organizations. Most of the fund-raising groups had been formed to aid orphans and poor families back in the immigrants' home countries of Europe. In addition to making a profit on the tickets, the charities often took up collections during the intermissions. The actors and theater managers allowed the extra speeches and the passing of the clinking coin boxes because the theater parties assured them of well-filled houses.

Second Avenue, though, wasn't for Jewish theatergoers only. American stage and film stars came to Second Avenue to see what its "Sweetheart," Molly Picon, and its other stars were all about. Even Jimmy Walker, the popular mayor of New York City, made an appearance at one of Molly's shows.

After the performance, Molly and Yonkel would take the visiting celebrities out to one of the famous eating places in the neighborhood—a kosher delicatessen or a

*At the Café Royal, Yiddish-theater people relaxed,
gossiped, and talked business.*

Romanian-style restaurant—where all the meats served
had been slaughtered and prepared in keeping with
Jewish dietary laws. Everybody loved the kosher "delis"
with their hot pastrami sandwiches and generous bowls
of free sauerkraut and pickles. Or one could sample a
kosher dairy restaurant, where no meats were ever
served because of the religious rules forbidding meat
and milk products at the same meal. Among the most
popular of the Russian-Jewish dairy dishes were blin-
tzes, very thin pancakes wrapped around a filling of
delicately flavored cheese and topped with sour cream.

The Yiddish-theater people themselves often gath-
ered after a performance at one of the club-like local
cafés. Until it closed its doors in 1945, the Café Royal on

Second Avenue was the favorite place for a little food, something to drink, and lots of "inside" gossip and deal-making.

As Molly's fame grew, it was almost to be expected that she would be invited into the world of American entertainment that lay beyond Second Avenue. So it wasn't surprising that in the spring of 1929 she received an offer to "play the Palace."

The Palace was the renowned vaudeville theater uptown in the Broadway entertainment district. The top singers and comedians of the day headlined there. It was a far cry from the vaudeville-circuit houses Molly had played in her early stint with "The Four Seasons." And the beginning salary was a staggering $2500 a week!

With her usual enthusiasm and optimism, and with Yonkel's support, Molly accepted the offer and set about adapting her material for an English-speaking audience. She also composed new songs and sketches and added a delightful imitation of Charlie Chaplin. Molly's devoted "downtown" followers came to see her, mingling with her new Broadway audiences, and she was a hit with both.

The timing had been lucky for Molly. In October 1929 the stock market crashed, ushering in the Great Depression of the 1930s. As unemployment increased, theater attendance dropped. But at least Molly had two stage careers. She was able to straddle successfully the worlds of both Yiddish theater and American vaudeville, playing engagements at home in New York and as far afield as London, Paris, South America, and even Palestine (later to become the State of Israel).

31

In 1933, after returning from entertaining both *kibbutzniks* (farming-settlement Jews) and Arabs in Palestine, Molly made her first talking picture. Although it seems to have been lost to history, it was soon to be followed by others. And in 1934, Molly and Yonkel began their first five-day-a-week radio talk show. It was a mix of songs, stories, and chitchat in both Yiddish and English. The sponsor was Jell-O.

Nobody could say that "Baby Margaret," who had grown up to be the "Sweetheart of Second Avenue," wasn't moving right along with the times.

4

Yiddel with His Fiddle

Molly was thirty-eight years old in 1936. But she was still playing yeshiva boys and "little mothers," children in their early teens. Suppose she was to make a movie of herself in such a role, one that would capture on film the antics and winning ways of her ever-youthful "Jewish Peter Pan" character?

The idea seemed too good to pass up. A Hollywood producer, Joseph Green, arranged with Yonkel to bring Molly to Poland to make a Yiddish-language musical to be titled *Yidl mitn Fidl*, or *Yiddel* (meaning "little Jewish boy") *with His Fiddle*.

Green chose to make the movie in Poland, the actual setting of the story, rather than in Hollywood, because production costs would be lower. And the "on-location" background of a real Polish-Jewish village would be far

Filming the village wedding scene in Yiddel with His Fiddle

more convincing than a Hollywood back lot. Besides, the film itself was intended mainly for the millions of Yiddish-speaking Jews all over Europe who had never seen a movie in their own language.

The story of *Yiddel* suited Molly perfectly. It was about a girl who has to dress up in boy's clothing so that she can travel with her wandering-musician father and his troupe through the towns and villages of Poland. As Yiddel and the others go from place to place, playing in courtyards and village squares for whatever coins are tossed to them, "Yiddel" begins to fall in love with a handsome young musician in the group. How can she, dressed as a rough

34

little scamp, let him know that she is really a young girl, bursting with tender feelings for him?

Kazimierz was the name of the small Jewish village, or *shtetl*, where *Yiddel* was filmed. Poor and shabby, it was typical of hundreds of other Jewish towns in Eastern Europe. Molly was deeply saddened by the tumble-down little houses and the pinched faces and broken shoes of the village children.

But Molly was also aware that something worse than poverty had begun to loom over the Jews of Poland, as well as other parts of Europe. A few years earlier, in 1933, Adolf Hitler had come to power in neighboring Germany.

The German dictator was making speech after speech in which he called the Jews an inferior race and insisted that Germany and all of Europe must rid itself of them.

Most people in 1936 still thought that Hitler was a madman and that his hysterical ravings would come to nothing. But Molly had run into anti-Semitism, hatred of Jews, in her own life. And she knew that among many people anti-Jewish feelings smoldered just beneath the surface, ready to be fanned into angry flames. Riding through Germany by train on her way to Poland, Molly had only to look out the window to see the red flags, with their large black swastikas against a white background, that were the banners of Hitler's Nazi party. Even children waved the swastika symbol. And already Jewish businesses had been boycotted and Jews had been stripped of their rights as German citizens.

In the excitement of making *Yiddel* in Kazimierz, one could almost forget the fearful events that were taking place back in Germany. The highlight of the film was a wedding scene in which almost the entire village took part. Mountains of real, kosher food were served to the villagers, who were playing the part of wedding guests. As the wedding scene had to be shot more than once, the festive meal went on and on. Most of the townspeople of Kazimierz hadn't ever *seen* a movie before, much less appeared in one. So they were a bit puzzled by the goings-on. But none failed to enjoy the delicious banquet, which had been ordered by the film's producer from the most famous kosher caterer in Warsaw, the Polish capital.

Yiddel with His Fiddle became a classic film. Not only did it show Molly off as both a lively urchin and a winning young woman. It also caught and preserved a rich glimpse of Jewish *shtetl* life as it had existed for hundreds of years—and was shortly to vanish forever. Today *Yiddel* is still being shown in America, Israel, and many other parts of the world. It is valued both as entertainment and as a rare historical record. If not for Molly's special talent for the role of Yiddel, the film might never have been made.

Two years later, in 1938, Molly was back in Poland to make yet another Yiddish-language film. This one was the movie version of the play, *Mamele*, in which Molly had starred so successfully back in the early 1920s. Molly was now forty years old. It would be much harder to look youthful in front of a movie camera than from behind the footlights on a theater stage. Could Molly really play a twelve-year-old girl?

Molly's makeup and costuming and the camera crew's lighting and lenses were chosen with care. But, in the end, the real triumph was Molly's. She knew how to put herself into the role so that the years dropped away as if by magic. She was "Mamele" once again, the little-girl "mother" of her family.

Mamele was one of the last of a number of Yiddish-language films that Joseph Green and others made in Poland in the late 1930s. By 1938, Hitler's power had grown enormously. He had annexed the neighboring country of Austria and turned it into a Nazi camp in which Jews were marked and terrorized. In a window-smashing, looting, and burning rampage known as *Kristallnacht*, or "Night of Broken Glass," Nazi mobs in both Germany and Austria destroyed Jewish shops, synagogues, and homes.

Molly as Mamele, *the twelve-year-old little mother*

The following year, 1939, Hitler invaded first Czecho-slovakia and then Poland. Both England and France had treaties with Poland. At once, they declared war on Germany. World War II had broken out. But it would be six long years before the Nazis would be defeated.

In that time, Jews in Europe would be systematically rounded up and sent to concentration camps where most would be killed. Six million were to die in history's most terrifying nightmare-come-true. Today that anni-hilation of the Jews is known as the Holocaust.

Back home in America, Molly felt helpless. Many European Jews had tried to escape the Nazis and their supporters. But only a very few were admitted to the United States. The restrictive immigration laws of the 1920s were still in effect. Some refugee Jews who arrived by ship, hoping for special permission to land, were actually turned away and sent back to Europe. The "golden door," through which so many immigrants had passed in the early 1900s, was no longer open.

Molly could read the handwriting on the wall. With so many of the world's Yiddish-speaking Jews facing destruction, the language itself was almost certain to die with time. Along with it would go the Yiddish theater.

The war years brought a little of everything to Molly and Yonkel, some of it very grim. In 1941 Yonkel's mother died in the ghetto of the Polish city of Lodz. The ghetto was a walled neighborhood, within the city, where the Nazis forced the Jews to live. They were crowded into cramped quarters and were slowly starved. Eventually the ghetto was emptied out and its remaining Jews were sent to the death camps.

In the following year, 1942, Papa Picon died. Molly's

father had continued to live away from the family and Molly was saddened at having to say good-bye to a man she had never really known.

On a happier note, Molly and Yonkel became foster parents to a Belgian-Jewish war orphan who had been rescued and brought to London. He was the first of four such young people who Molly and Yonkel were to take into their home at various times and of whom they would be proud. Also, Molly did her first English-speaking dramatic role on Broadway in a play called *Morning Star*. And she gave Broadway its first Yiddish-English musical *Oy, Is Dus a Leben*, or *Oh, What a Life*.

In *Morning Star*, Molly played a "grown-up" Jewish mother named Becky Felderman who is struggling to raise her children alone during the early 1900s. The part called for Molly to age twenty years during the story, playing an older rather than younger part for once. The reviewers admired Molly as the widowed Becky. But they didn't think much of the play beyond saying it was "friendly and likable." It ran for only eight weeks, too short a time to be a big success by Broadway standards.

Oy, Is Dus a Leben did much better. It had been written and directed by Yonkel, and it was actually Molly's life story from the time she had appeared as a child actress, through her marriage, her travels, and her climb to stardom on Second Avenue. For 139 performances, Molly relived her own life on the stage. Even the Broadway theater in which *Oy, Is Dus a Leben* was presented had been renamed in Molly's honor. Once known as the Al Jolson Theatre, it was now called the Molly Picon.

During the remainder of the war years, Molly was taken up with vaudeville tours and especially with entertaining the men and women of the armed services. The United States had entered the war in 1941, and there were military training camps throughout the country. Molly also appeared at bond rallies, offering her talents to raise money for the war effort. Through most of this period, she and Yonkel also managed to continue their daily radio show, which was now being sponsored by Maxwell House Coffee.

At last, in May of 1945, Germany was defeated and the war in Europe ended. Hitler had taken his own life, still ranting against the Jews and blaming them for the war. The Allied armies that invaded German-held Europe liberated the handfuls of survivors from the concentration camps. And the unspeakable crimes of the Nazis were revealed for all the world to see.

The dead were recalled by piles of corpses. The camps were also found to contain warehouses filled with human belongings, even with hair shaved from the heads of the doomed, which was used by the Germans to stuff mattresses. The living stumbled about, dazed human skeletons, homeless and dressed in rags.

On learning of these conditions, Molly and Yonkel had but one thought. They wanted to go to Europe as soon as possible, paying their own way if necessary, bringing small gifts for the refugees, and giving free performances in the concentration camps, which had now been converted into "displaced persons" camps.

Molly and Yonkel announced their plans on their radio show and in newspapers like *Variety*, which carried all the news of show business. They received many donations of food and other needed items for the survivors of the Nazi atrocities.

Much of the Europe they would visit was bombed-out, its people haunted by the ravages of war. Molly knew that the journey would be filled with hardships and scenes of great sadness. But her mission filled her with energy and hope. More than anything else, she wanted to bring the gift of laughter to the broken lives and spirits of the victims of Nazism.

5

Milk and Honey

Molly and Yonkel set sail for Europe on a crowded, uncomfortable ship that was very different from the passenger liners on which they had crossed the Atlantic before the war. It was now May of 1946, a year since the Germans had surrendered. But permission to travel to the war zones had been very difficult to get. Molly and Yonkel were among the first American entertainers to visit the camps, hospitals, and orphanages of the homeless.

Molly had thought long and hard about what gifts she could bring to people who for so many years had lived without the barest necessities. The trunks, valises, and duffel bags she took aboard ship with her were filled, of course, with essential food and medical supplies. But Molly had also wanted to bring along some luxuries that

*Molly and Yonkel packed hundreds of gifts
for the survivors of the concentration camps.*

women might enjoy. So she wrapped hundreds of little packages in colorful paper. Inside them were lipsticks, costume jewelry, and other small items to cheer the grim lives of the refugees. And, naturally, she and Yonkel traveled with plenty of chocolate bars for the children.

After landing in France, Molly and Yonkel eventually made their way east to Poland and Czechoslovakia. With horror, they viewed the rubble of Warsaw and of the city's ghetto where the last of the trapped Jews had bravely tried to revolt against the Nazi authorities. The uprising had failed and nearly all of the 400,000 Jews who had originally been placed in the ghetto had been killed, most of them in the death camps. Molly and Yonkel also visited the camps themselves.

After sights too terrible to bear, they turned their attention to setting up their concerts on makeshift stages in barracks halls and open fields. Their audiences included orphaned children, men and women who had been forcibly separated from their families, people of all ages hoping against hope that they might still be reunited with vanished loved ones.

Molly was determined to bring these people a few moments of pleasure, the promise that there might still be some happiness in their lives. She bounced brightly onto the stage and went into her act of Yiddish songs and stories, dance routines and somersaults. These were antics that always warmed her audiences' hearts, made their eyes sparkle, and brought laughter to their lips. But this time something was wrong.

People sat quietly watching. Why was it so hard to coax laughter from them? What was Molly doing wrong?

She was soon to learn that the fault wasn't hers. It was simply that many of the survivors had forgotten *how* to laugh. For years, they had known only fear, cruelty, and loss. They had become numb. Even sadder, there were refugee children born during the war who had *never* known the sound of laughter.

Molly realized that just as food must be fed gradually to the starving, pleasure is slower in coming to those whose emotions have been deadened. This was why her gift of laughter was received slowly at first. But even the most broken-spirited could not resist Molly. And before long she had one after another of her audiences clapping their hands and shouting for "More!"

In the city of Lodz, in Poland, Yonkel made inquiries about his mother who had died in the ghetto. He and

Molly were relieved to learn that the eighty-three-year-old woman had died of natural causes, before the ghetto inhabitants had been rounded up and sent to the camps. But, sadly, her grave could not be found, for the Jewish cemeteries had been destroyed.

For nearly five months, Molly and Yonkel traveled through war-torn Europe, putting up with hard beds, bumpy roads, and poor food. But these inconveniences were small compared with the sufferings of the surviving Jews. How would they re-establish their lives and build for the future? Hope seemed to rest now with the possible birth of a Jewish homeland in Palestine.

Back in America, Molly returned to her busy schedule of radio shows, theater performances, and concert tours, as well as writing much of her own material and learning new stage skills. At the age of fifty, Molly actually took up roller skating for the first time. It would be part of her act in an upcoming musical celebrating the twenty-fifth anniversary of her debut on Second Avenue. The play, written by Yonkel, was called *Abi Gezunt,* or *As Long as You're Healthy.*

There was also a new way for Molly to "meet" her audiences. It was called television. But, although she began making appearances on the small screen as early as 1948, Molly never felt completely happy with the new medium. She missed the instant feedback from the live theater audiences that she loved.

The year 1948 also brought an event of great importance to Jews all over the world. The independent State of Israel was proclaimed in Palestine. A year earlier Molly had written a stirring song called "We Shall Live to See the Day," foretelling the birth of Israel. Although

Israel's Arab neighbors opposed the creation of a Jewish state and immediately attacked it, Israel fought and won a war for its survival. Even though there would be future struggles, Molly's dream of a country to which all Jews would be freely admitted had at last come true.

Now Molly had a new activity to add to her career— that of raising money for the State of Israel through bond rallies. Unlike the old days on Second Avenue, Jewish audiences were now scattered in many parts of the country. So Molly traveled on her own bond-selling circuit, which included Florida where many Jews were now spending their winters.

As for Second Avenue, Molly's fears about a dying Yiddish theater were slowly coming true. The number of theater-goers was shrinking. Older people stopped coming because of age or ill health, and younger ones understood little or no Yiddish. Also, television was making inroads on live theater and movie-going in general. Many people preferred to be entertained in their own homes. It was cheaper than going out for the evening and besides no baby-sitters were needed.

Like every actor, Molly knew failures and disappointments in her career as well as successes. Her nightclub audiences were sometimes rowdy and even rude. Jewish audiences didn't always support the creation of a Jewish homeland; some thought it was better for Jews to be part of a world community. New plays were tried out and never opened. Or they were instant flops because of poor material, problems with cast members, lack of publicity, or bad reviews.

A particularly unhappy time for Molly came with the death of Mama Picon in the fall of 1953. While Papa had been almost a stranger to Molly, Mama had been a guiding and loving force in her life. Mama's encouragement went all the way back to that day on the trolley in 1903 when she had prompted Molly to give a dress rehearsal of her amateur-night recitation, "I'm Afraid to Go Home in the Dark." Mama had truly been both mother *and* father to Molly, so her loss was doubly felt.

But in spite of her deep sadness, Molly remembered the first rule of the theater—"the show must go on." And, fortunately, new experiences and glowing stage triumphs still lay ahead for Molly.

In 1955, she and Yonkel made the first of many trips to the State of Israel. Molly had entertained in the land of Palestine way back in 1933. Now it was the site of a brave new nation, the home of many wartime refugees, yet bursting with youthful energy. In appreciation of all that Molly and Yonkel had done in support of Israel, the new government received them as honored guests.

World hopes for the future of the Jewish homeland were great. So it wasn't surprising that a few years later the Broadway composer, Jerry Herman, was inspired to write a musical play with an Israeli setting. Herman first planned to call the play *Shalom!*, for this is Israel's traditional Hebrew greeting meaning "Hello," "Goodbye," and—above all—"Peace."

But soon the title was changed to *Milk and Honey*, reflecting the settlers' dream of making their desert land rich and fruitful. The music included lively horas and other folk dances. And right on the New York stage there were scenes of Israeli farming life including a real tractor, bales of hay, and a live goat that was milked at every performance.

Molly in the goat-milking scene from Milk and Honey

The story was about a group of American women tourists who visit the newly created State of Israel, and especially about two of them who fall in love there. Who else but Molly was chosen to play the leading comedy role? And, of course, as the wisecracking widow with all the funny lines, Molly practically stole the show.

When Clara Weiss, the character Molly played, fell in love, she sang a comical yet touching number called a "Hymn to Hymie" that Molly herself had written. In the song, the widow asks her long-dead husband, Hymie, for permission to marry again. And Molly's pert, twinkle-toed character does indeed marry her new-found love.

Milk and Honey was Molly's first appearance—at the age of sixty-three—in a Broadway musical. The portrayal of Israel in *Milk and Honey* was, of course, overly romantic. And the play's love story was sentimental and even a little silly. The real Israel was much less glamorous. It was a nation striving for development and desperately anxious about its security.

Still, the play attracted large audiences and was a long-running hit. For Molly, though, it was much more than a theatrical success. She could vividly recall the despair she had felt in 1946 upon visiting the displaced-persons camps of Europe. Now, in 1961, the very fact that a play with an Israeli setting had been produced on Broadway marked the great changes that had since come about. And Molly's concern for the future of the world's Jews had been transformed into hope.

6

Matchmaker, Matchmaker

In 1969, Molly and Yonkel celebrated their fiftieth wedding anniversary. Half a century had passed since Molly had been stranded in Boston with "The Four Seasons" vaudeville act, met Yonkel, and married him in the back room of Mama Picon's little Philadelphia grocery store.

Molly often mused on their relationship, which had been much more than a long, happy marriage. Yonkel had guided Molly into the Yiddish theater when it was in its heyday. He had written most of her material and had helped to raise her to stardom. From Second Avenue she had gone on to make an impressive Broadway debut and to perform her numerous roles on tour both at home and abroad. Occasionally she and Yonkel even acted opposite each other. Their union truly seemed to have been made by some kind of heavenly matchmaker.

The very next year, in 1970, Molly herself was offered the chance to act the part of a matchmaker. It was to be in a movie version of the musical play *Fiddler on the Roof*, which had been a record-breaking stage success on Broadway and on tour since its opening in 1964.

Fiddler was based on the stories of the famed Yiddish writer, Sholem Aleichem. It took place in a tiny Russian village called Anatevka in the year 1905. Among the main characters were Tevye, a poor dairyman; his wife, Golde; and their five daughters. And—as arranged marriages were the custom in that time and place—there was a matchmaker in the story. Her name was Yente.

Molly was a natural choice for Yente, and she accepted the role with pleasure. She could be both funny and bossy as the little old lady who controlled the futures of Tevye's daughters and of other young women with her matchmaking. Yonkel, too, had a part in *Fiddler*. He played a *melamed*, a teacher of children, wearing a beard that he had grown especially for his first movie appearance.

There was no way, of course, to shoot the movie in a real *shtetl* like Sholem Aleichem's Anatevka. All of the old Jewish villages of Eastern Europe had vanished since World War II. So Molly and Yonkel and the rest of the cast traveled to Yugoslavia. There, the "on-location" scenes were filmed in a village that was amazingly similar to a Jewish *shtetl*, with peasant houses, geese wandering in the lanes, and streets of mud. Actually, Molly's classic movie *Yiddel with His Fiddle*, made in 1936, served to show *Fiddler*'s director what such a village should look like.

Although the movie version of *Fiddler* received mixed reviews, Molly was praised by the prominent film critic of *The New York Times*. He found her interpretation of the matchmaker to be "the single most touching performance

Molly and Yonkel pose together during a rehearsal break for the film Fiddler on the Roof.

in the film," calling it "authentic," "entertaining," and "very dear."

Yet Molly had been relieved when the many months of filming came to an end. They were a trying time, especially as Yonkel's health had begun to fail. Unlike stage plays, movies are put together in bits and pieces, and in no special order. Often an actor sits around in makeup and costume for days without ever being called on to do a scene. Sometimes actors who play in different scenes of the same movie never even meet one another.

Molly had made her first Hollywood movie in 1962. It starred Frank Sinatra and was called *Come Blow Your Horn*. Molly had played Frank's Jewish mother! And a few years after *Fiddler*, in 1973, Molly made a picture with Barbra Streisand called *For Pete's Sake*. But, whether shooting a film in Hollywood or anywhere else, Molly missed the electricity of a live theater audience.

The same continued to be true of her many television appearances. She was on talk shows hosted by Merv Griffin, Mike Douglas, Jack Paar, Johnny Carson, and others. And she acted in segments of popular TV series. But even when there was a studio audience present, Molly felt less than satisfied working in front of a camera.

So, even as the years kept adding up for Molly, she went on performing in revivals of old plays and tryouts of new ones, and giving live concert performances. In her mid-seventies, she could still do deep knee-bends and cancan twirls. In interviews about her ongoing energy and bounciness, Molly was often quoted as saying that they were the result of "genes and luck."

A temporary halt came for Molly, however, with the

growing seriousness of Yonkel's illness. And, in 1975, after a period of great suffering, her beloved Yonkel died. The despair that Molly felt after fifty-six years of sharing with him both a marriage and a life in the theater seemed overwhelming.

Molly could remember picking herself up and going onstage to do a "bonds for Israel" concert almost immediately after Mama had died. But now, for the first time, she wondered if she would again be able to "go on with the show."

She knew, though, that Yonkel would have wanted her to continue. And slowly she began to put the pieces of her life together again. One of the most healing experiences was the writing of her life story. Yonkel himself had been planning to undertake a biography of Molly for a very long time. Now Molly would complete his work . . . and her own.

For years, Molly had kept diaries, collected anecdotes, given interviews, issued press releases, and saved clippings of reviews and comments on her professional career. She compiled all of this into a warm, chatty autobiography that was called simply *Molly!* Her book delighted her readers almost as much as Molly herself had delighted her audiences for seventy-five years on the stage.

Even before the book's publication took place in 1980, Molly had found her way back into the theater. In April 1979, she gave an especially memorable performance. She was featured in a one-woman show at the Eighth Annual Sholem Aleichem Festival of the Jewish Arts, at New York City's Queens College.

To Molly's surprise, she was asked to do her show in

Yiddish. Queens College had four hundred students of Yiddish language who were determined to keep alive the tongue that most people feared was dying. And there would be many others at the performance who felt as the students did. So Molly brushed up on her Yiddish and dusted off her *Yonkele* costume for the "Jewish Peter Pan" role that she had played 3000 times!

Before a packed house, filled with both young and old, a sprightly eighty-one-year-old Molly again became *Yonkele*, the yeshiva boy. She also told jokes and stories, danced, and sang songs she was famous for, including "The Story of Grandma's Shawl," "The Working Girl," and "We Shall Live to See the Day." It had often been said of Molly that she was a failure at only one thing— retirement. Once more she had proven that this was so.

At eighty-three, the miraculous Molly—still giving about thirty concerts a year—was elected to the Theater Hall of Fame. On a list of twenty-six names of famous theater figures, she was the only actress who had also performed on the Yiddish stage. To be eligible for membership, one had to have a major career of at least twenty-five years on Broadway alone. Molly more than qualified.

A few years later, in 1985, Molly received a Yiddish-theater award that had only just been created, almost surely with her in mind. The award, known as a Goldie, was comparable to an Oscar, a Tony, or an Obie—established awards given for prize-winning Hollywood, Broadway, or off-Broadway contributions. The Goldie statuette was sculpted in the likeness of Abraham Goldfadn, a playwright known as the "father of the Yiddish theater."

Molly was now in her late eighties. Perhaps the time

Molly, as she will always be remembered

had come at last for her to do the one thing she had so far failed at. Perhaps it was, after all, time to retire.

There was much for Molly to look back on with deep satisfaction. She had been a beloved entertainer on theater stages all over the world, ranging from the famed Broadway Palace to drab army bases and makeshift platforms in the refugee camps of war-torn Europe. Everywhere, she had lifted the spirits and captured the hearts of her audiences.

Through her talent, enthusiasm, and love of people, life had brought Molly many rewards. But greatest of all was the gift she had so generously bestowed on others— the gift of laughter.

IMPORTANT DATES IN THE LIFE OF MOLLY PICON

1898   Molly is born on Manhattan's Lower East Side. June 1 is observed as her date of birth. Some years later, a birth certificate is issued indicating that she was born on February 28, 1898. Molly then celebrates *two* birthdays each year.

1903   Molly makes her stage debut at the age of five, winning a children's amateur-night contest at the Bijou Theatre in Philadelphia.

1915   Molly leaves William Penn High School in Philadelphia to follow a full-time stage career.

1919   Molly marries Jacob Kalich (Yonkel) on June 29 in Philadelphia.

1923   After two years of performing Yiddish theater in Europe, Molly makes a successful debut on Second Avenue in New York City.

1929   Molly bows in American vaudeville at Broadway's Palace Theatre.

1934   Molly and Yonkel begin their first daily radio show.

1936   Molly makes the film *Yiddel with His Fiddle*, in Poland.

1938   On the eve of World War II (1939–1945), Molly makes a second film *Mamele*, in Poland.

1940   Molly appears in *Morning Star*, her first English-language dramatic role on Broadway.

1942   Molly's father, Louis Picon, dies.

1946   Molly and Yonkel spend five months in postwar Europe, where Molly entertains at displaced-persons camps.

1948   Molly makes her first appearance on American television.

1949   Molly celebrates twenty-five years on the Yiddish stage with a new play on Second Avenue, *Abi Gezunt.*

1953   Molly's mother, Clara Ostrow Picon, dies.

1955   Molly and Yonkel make their first visit to the State of Israel, which had come into existence in 1948.

1961   Molly opens in her first Broadway musical *Milk and Honey.*

1962   Molly makes her first Hollywood movie *Come Blow Your Horn,* starring Frank Sinatra.

1969   Molly and Yonkel celebrate their fiftieth wedding anniversary.

1971   The movie version of *Fiddler on the Roof* is released, with Molly in the role of Yente, the matchmaker.

1973   Molly appears in the Hollywood movie *For Pete's Sake,* starring Barbra Streisand.

1975   Yonkel dies on March 16, after a long illness.

1979   Molly performs a one-woman show in Yiddish at the Eighth Annual Sholem Aleichem Festival at Queens College.

1980   *Molly!*, the autobiography of Molly Picon, is published.

1981   Molly is elected to Broadway's Theater Hall of Fame.

1985   Molly is one of the first three Yiddish-theater stars to be honored with a Goldie, a newly created annual award for contributions to Jewish culture.

AUTHOR'S NOTE

About writing *Molly Picon: A Gift of Laughter*

In my family, in the years when I was growing up, Molly Picon's name was a household word. My parents and grandparents attended many of her performances and spoke of her with admiration, love, and even a kind of family pride. I have seen Molly Picon perform in films only, but so much of her vivacity and warmth have been conveyed to me that I almost feel that I, too, have experienced her "live."

Molly Picon's career seems to me to have a dual significance. In addition to being a luminous theater personality who brought joy and laughter to so many, she was a vibrant figure in Jewish life and culture. Her work in the Yiddish theater immediately following the peak years of Jewish immigration to America, her filmmaking in prewar Poland on the eve of the Holocaust, her postwar visits to the displaced-persons camps of Eastern Europe, her bond rallies in support of the State of Israel— all of these link her to some eighty years of turbulent Jewish history and development.

Always generous with anecdotes and information about herself, Molly Picon gave many interviews to the press over the years. And her work in the theater was, of course, a matter of record. I am especially grateful to the New York Public Library for the use of the Molly Picon clipping file in the Billy Rose Theatre Collection at the Lincoln Center Library. Among the hundreds of documents consulted were newspaper and magazine clippings, press releases, and theater programs.

My journalistic sources included *The New York Times, New York Post, New York World-Telegram, New York World-Telegram and Sun, New York Herald Tribune, New York Morning Telegraph, New York Daily News, New York Sunday News, New York Mirror, Variety, Long Island Press, Westport Fair Press* (Connecticut), *Westport News* (Connecticut), *Boston Globe,* and *Washington Post.*

Among encyclopedias consulted were *Who's Who in the Theatre,* 1947; *Current Biography,* 1951; *Encyclopedia of American Theatre,* 1900–1975; *Judaica Encyclopedia,* Volume 13, 1971; *Who's Who in the Theatre,* 17th Edition, 1981; and *Contemporary Authors,* Volume 104, 1982. For background material on the Yiddish theater, I am indebted to *Vagabond Stars: A World History of Yiddish Theater* by Nahma Sandrow, published in 1977 by Harper and Row.

Molly!, Molly Picon's autobiography written with Jean Bergantini Grillo and published by Simon and Schuster in 1980, explored in depth much of the widely documented material that the author had long shared with her public. Written with lively humor, folksy warmth, and unrestrained enthusiasm, *Molly!* also delightfully transmitted the author's loving and gallant spirit. I am grateful, along with her numerous other readers, for this rich summing up of her life and career in her own words.

INDEX